Gen 7: 25 —

When, God, When?

Deut 25: 17

Ch

2 he

Stress   Is 57: 10

James 3. 13 —
      4: 10

Grace like Manna
 Cannot be stored up.
Ex 16: 15 —
Psalm 37: 3 + 4

When, God, When?

Learning To Trust
In God's Timing

by
Joyce Meyer

Harrison House
Tulsa, Oklahoma

10th Printing

When, God, When?
Learning To Trust in God's Timing
ISBN 0-89274-846-X
Copyright © 1994 by Joyce Meyer
Life In The Word, Inc.
P. O. Box 655
Fenton, Missouri 63026

Published by Harrison House, Inc.
P. O. Box 35035
Tulsa, Oklahoma 74153

Contents

Foreword

We serve the All-Knowing God who keeps an eye on us all the time. God is never surprised. He knows everything *before* it happens. Psalm 139 says He knows our thoughts before we think them, and our yet unuttered words. Most of us need to grow in the area of trust and attempt to silence the big question – WHEN?

Because that question is a persistent one, I have written this book to bring some insight that I feel God has graciously shared with me. I spent a large part of my life impatient, frustrated, and disappointed. Through many experiences, I have learned to trust the One Who knows all.

I pray your spirit will become peaceful as you rest in Him, trusting that, in the words of King David, "your times are in His very capable hands" (Ps. 31:15, paraphrased).

1

Timing and Trust

"I trusted in, relied on, and was confident in You, O Lord; I said, You are my God.

"My times are in Your hands; deliver me from the hands of my foes and those who pursue me and persecute me."

Psalm 31:14,15 AMP

In this chapter the Psalmist is saying that he trusted God to deliver him, and he trusted Him to do it at the right time. Trust requires us to say, "*My times* are in *Your hands*" (paraphrase).

I have learned that trust requires us to accept that some questions will be unanswered and to place our times in God's hands – believing that even though we do not know all the answers, He does.

He has a perfect timing for all things in our lives. We all desire and believe for good things to happen in our lives, NOW – *not later*!

As we continuously mature in the Christian life, we learn to believe for things not *NOW*, but in God's perfect timing. Hebrews 11:1 says, "NOW faith is the substance of things hoped for, the evidence of things not seen." We can always have faith now, but we cannot always have the manifestation *now*.

Trusting God often requires not knowing *how* God is going to accomplish what needs to be done and not knowing *when* He will do it. We always say, "God is never late," but He is generally not early either. Why? Because He uses those opportunities to stretch our faith in Him, and we grow during times of waiting.

One of our partners recently was in need of financial help from God in paying some unexpected taxes. The taxes were due April 15. The couple gave a special offering to Life In The Word believing

God for the miracle they needed. On April 14 they had the money for their taxes. Why not April 1 or 5? Why does God sometimes wait until the very last day or minute?

The reason is that He is teaching us lessons in trust! *Trust is not inherited; it is learned!* We learn to trust God by going through various experiences that require trust. By seeing God's faithfulness over and over, we let go of trusting ourselves, and gradually we enter God's rest and place our trust in Him.

Looking at it like this, it is easy to see how timing plays an important part in learning to trust God. If He did everything we asked for immediately, we would never grow and develop. Timing and trust are twins. They work side by side.

2

. . . .

Due Season

Leviticus 26:4 says, "I will give you rain in *due season*." Galatians 6:9 (AMP) says we must ". . . not lose heart and grow weary and faint in acting nobly and doing right, for in due time and at the appointed season we shall reap, if we do not loosen and relax our courage and faint." And in First Peter 5:6 we are exhorted to "humble" [ourselves] "under the mighty hand of God, that in *due time* He may exalt" [us].

When is *due season* or *due time*? I believe it is when God knows we are ready, when everyone else involved is ready and when it fits into God's corporate plan. God has an individual plan for our individual lives, but He also has a corporate plan for the entire world.

I remember a time when I was frustrated because nothing was

happening in my ministry I knew I was anointed to teach God's Word, but absolutely no doors opened for me. It seemed I had waited so long. I felt ready. I had been cooperating with God. He had done major work in me, and I just could not understand why something was not happening. I remember asking, "God, what are You waiting for now? Am I not ready yet?" He responded by saying, "You are, but some of the others who will be involved with you are not yet ready, and I am still working some things out in them, so you will have to wait on them now."

You see, God does not push, shove, demand, manipulate or force people. He leads, guides, prompts and suggests. It is the responsibility of each person to give his or her will over to Him for His purposes. Sometimes this takes longer with one person than another.

Therefore, if God is developing a group of people or a team of people who will work together, part of them may be ready before the rest. This is especially hard, since at the birthing stage, they generally do not know God's plan, and many times they do not even yet know each other.

An excellent example of this is the single person praying for the perfect mate. God is, in fact, preparing that mate, but the one praying gets tired of waiting since they do not know what is going on behind the scenes. The single person praying for a mate who is already a mature Christian, developed in the fruit of the Spirit and called into full-time ministry, etc., may need to be willing to wait to get their "special order" all fixed up on arrival. That takes time. It does not happen overnight. However, God has the right person for them.

Dave got me quickly, but his was not a demanding prayer. He asked God for a wife, the right one for him, and he asked God for her to be someone who needed help. He prayed on and off for approximately six months to one year. We met, had five dates and got married. We have been married twenty-eight years as of the publishing of this book in 1994. Dave has always said he knew I was the right one the first night we went out, but he waited to ask me to marry him because he did not want to frighten me.

He arrived at the conclusion, after only three weeks of marriage, that I had quite a few problems and was in need of much help. Dave received the answer to his prayer quickly, but he also had to endure a lot of hard times while I was growing up in God and overcoming the problems from my abusive past.

God knew that Dave was mature enough to handle the rough years with me; therefore, He answered Dave's prayer quickly. He was strong enough to help someone who had many problems. Dave was willing to be used by God in that way, and God used him. Had he been unable to handle it or if he had prayed for someone more perfected, I believe God would have delayed His answer until a more appropriate time, after the Lord had done some major things in my life to get me to the place Dave had requested.

The point I am trying to make is that when we are waiting on God, it is essential that we realize that God may be working out some things with several people in order to answer our prayer. Believing that makes waiting more endurable.

Let us think about *due time* in regard to financial increase. Third John 2 says, "Beloved, I wish above all things that thou mayest prosper and be in health, even as thy soul prospereth." The phrase *even as your soul prospers* lets us know that God's prosperity depends upon our maturity. *As your soul prospers* refers to how fast we allow God to bring our mind, will and emotions into line with His will.

Maturity is a process that takes time. How much time it takes is dependent upon God's plan and how well we cooperate with that plan. God loves us too much to give us prosperity that we would not be mature enough to handle properly. Therefore, He tells us, in Galatians 6:9, "Let us not be weary in well doing: for in due season we shall reap, if we faint not." *Due season* is when God knows we are ready, not when we *think* we are ready.

Too many blessings too soon can make a person haughty, thus the Bible instructs us not to place a novice or a new convert in leadership. They are not mature enough, and it would cause them to be lifted up in pride. (1 Tim. 3:6.)

There is a timing for all things in our lives, and there is *safety* in being in God's perfect timing. I pray to be in God's perfect will and His perfect timing – not one step ahead of Him, nor one step behind.

3

....

Appointed Time

Jesus told the disciples in Acts 1:6-8, when they asked Him questions concerning the end times, that it was not for them to know what time would bring and the seasons which the Father had *appointed* by His own choice and personal power.

You see, the disciples still thought Jesus would set up an earthly kingdom. They asked when He would re-establish the kingdom and restore it to Israel.

Jesus had been unable to get them to understand that He was going to establish a spiritual kingdom and that His kingdom would be within them. The Bible warns us that knowledge without wisdom is dangerous. It would have been disastrous for Jesus to tell the disciples when He would establish the kingdom since they did not even understand what it was.

Many times we want information on *when*, and God cannot give it because we do not have enough wisdom to handle the knowledge. Habakkuk 2:3 (AMP) says, "For the vision is yet for an appointed time and it hastens to the end [fulfillment]; it will not deceive or disappoint. Though it tarry, wait [earnestly] for it, because it will surely come; it will not be behindhand on its appointed day." It will not be late one single day.

Appointed time simply means when God knows the time is right. We must humble ourselves and our ideas to the wisdom and power of God and trust Him when He says He will not be late.

Appointed time also means a time already established and decided for certain reasons. *It is like having an appointment*. We cannot get in until the appointment time comes, and that is just the way it is. God has an appointed time, or we might say that He has set appointments for us concerning certain issues in our lives. We might as well settle down and wait patiently because that is when it will happen and not until then.

4

....

The Call

The timing involved when God calls a person to do a certain thing, then anoints them for it and further separates them to do the work can be, and usually is, at three different intervals. Often there are lengthy time spans between the three events, particularly if the person is going to be used by God in a major way. *Major* does not necessarily mean worldwide. It just means in a way that will affect a good number of people. In this and the next two chapters, we will look at each of these events separately.

When God places a call on someone's life, it can be something that comes suddenly, or it can be something that the person has somehow always known. I remember reading that one of the U.S. presidents had stated in an interview that from the time he was quite young, he had always had a desire and "just knew" that he would someday be the president of the United States.

My call came rather suddenly. I was making my bed one morning, and the voice of the Lord came unto me saying, "You are going to go all over the place and teach my Word, and you are going to have a large teaching tape ministry." Even though it was not an audible voice, it sounded quite loud and clear inside me. And from that moment on, I "just knew" that was my destiny, and I had a tremendous, often overwhelming desire to teach the Word.

I never knew before that day that I was called to preach and teach God's Word. However, I can look back now and see other signposts along the way in my life. I always had an ability to express myself verbally and in writing in a very clear, understandable manner. People came to me even in high school for help and counseling with their problems. I had a desire even then to help people straighten out their lives. I was even asked to give the commencement address at my high school graduation to motivate and prod my classmates on to greater things. I even contemplated going to school to obtain a degree in psychology so I that could help people as a profession.

After Dave and I had been married for several years, I was growing closer to the Lord but still struggling with tremendous problems in my life because of my abusive past. We had three children by this time, and I remember coming home from church and lying in bed on Sunday evenings after the kids were asleep. The house was peaceful, quiet and dark, and I would repreach the pastor's sermons, only it was me at the pulpit and not the pastor. I never had any idea why I did that, but now I know.

Your call may come gradually or suddenly, but from the time you are called, *you are in preparation.*

5

....

The Anointing

During the preparation time, the anointing is being released in perfectly timed capsules. The anointing is the Holy Spirit enabling us to do what God has called us to do. The Holy Spirit teaches, corrects, sanctifies, helps and strengthens us. He molds and fashions us into vessels fit for the Master's use. This can take years and years to accomplish.

Think of Moses. He was sensing a call on his life to deliver his people from bondage. He stepped out in zeal and killed an Egyptian who was mistreating an Israelite, and, as a result, he spent the next forty years on the back side of the desert learning about shepherding, getting to know God and being humbled. *He was gaining experience*. A person without training, experience and humility cannot distinguish the difference between zeal and God's timing.

The anointing is released in our lives according to how we cooperate with the preparation process. Consider Joseph, called by God to be a ruler in Egypt to save multitudes from starvation. He was having dreams about it as a young boy. In zeal, he told his dreams to his brothers. They were not exactly thrilled with the thought of bowing down to their younger brother, so they sold him.

Now Joseph did not mean any harm. He was a sweet boy, but he obviously did not use wisdom by telling them what he had seen in his dreams. God allowed some hard years in his life, but those years trained him in wisdom. His experiences prepared him for his life's call. He went through being betrayed by not only his family but also by friends he had treated well and thought he could trust. He was lied about, misjudged and punished for things of which he was not guilty, and he had to wait many years before he saw the fulfillment of his dreams.

We all have similar experiences in various ways that help us grow up. They prepare us to be in God's service and stand steadfast no matter what. God does not bring our trouble; Satan does. The devil has our destruction in mind, but God turns it around and uses it for our good. Joseph knew this as well because in Genesis 50:20 he told his repentant brothers, "What you intended for my harm, God meant for good" (paraphrased).

When God called me to teach His Word, I had family and friends reject me, and I was very lonely and hurt by it. I was misjudged, misunderstood and talked about unkindly. However, I was also presumptuous, impetuous and full of unwise zeal. In short, *I was full of myself*. I might add, everybody is until they go through the preparation process themselves.

Should you happen to be thinking, "Not me – I don't have these problems," I would suggest that you are in for a rude awakening about yourself! And until you "humble" yourself "under the mighty hand of God," your due time will never come. (1 Pet. 5:6.)

I can look back now and see very distinct stages of progress in my ministry that correlated with stages of personal growth and a greater anointing.

Home Bible Studies

In one of the first stages God instructed me to quit my well-paying, full-time job in order to prepare for ministry, which I finally did. This decision cut our income in half. God always met our needs, but those were lean years.

I began by teaching home Bible studies, which went on for about five years. During the first two and one-half years, I taught once a week. The meeting grew so large that I started teaching two meetings – one in the morning and the second in the evening. Even though Dave and I were experiencing severe financial stress at that time, I received nothing financially for those meetings.

The people we were teaching, about twenty-five at each meeting, resisted any idea of an offering being received for us even though we had some obvious needs. It was hard for me, but it purified my motives for teaching. I kept doing it, so I clearly was not doing it for money. Although it was difficult at times not to be resentful toward the people, I eventually learned that things were happening this way because God did not want me to know where my provision was going to come from. He wanted to establish *Himself* as my source, and this takes *time* as well as enduring hard situations we would like to run from.

Many do run. They are called, but because they are not willing to endure the preparation time, they are never chosen out from among the called. Matthew 20:16 (AMP) says, "Many are called, but few chosen." I heard one speaker say that this means "many are called, but few are

Gen 14:22-24
Abraham

willing to accept the responsibility for the call."

The Amplified Bible's translation of Second Timothy 2:15 expounds a little on the responsibility we have for the call, "Study and be eager and do your utmost to present yourself to God approved (tested by trial), a workman who has no cause to be ashamed, correctly analyzing and accurately dividing [rightly handling and skillfully teaching] the Word of Truth."

During those years of teaching in a living room to twenty-five people, God taught me a great deal about ministry.

Put On a Shelf

Then, I had one whole year in which I did absolutely nothing in ministry. God had spoken to me, saying, "Stop the home Bible studies; behold, I do a new thing." My desire to do the Bible studies had vanished! I had a new baby, and everything in my heart, as well as my circumstances, gave confirmation to that Word from God.

In one way, it was hard to obey. The people had finally begun to give us a small offering each week. It was usually somewhere between fifteen and fifty dollars. But over a month, it was helping us out a lot. Now I had to be willing to walk away from that source of provision in order to go on to the next step.

My flesh expected something grand to happen after my sacrificial obedience; however, *nothing happened for one year!* No doors opened! In many ways this was one of the hardest years of my life. Had I missed God? Had I made up my whole vision? Would it ever happen? What could I do to make it happen? God kept saying, "Be still, and know that I am God" (Ps. 46:10).

Sometimes it is so hard to wait and be still for God's timing. At the time I didn't understand what I am telling you about now. We have a much clearer understanding of things when we look back on them and far less understanding while we are pressing through them.

Sometimes God puts people on a shelf and just lets them sit there. It seems as though nothing is happening, and yet much is being accomplished in the Spirit. It is a time of growth, fine-tuning, purifying and believing when there is nothing at all to see.

The Next Five Years

Toward the end of this year of waiting, Dave and I began attending a new church. It was just starting in the St. Louis area. It was small, about thirty people, but we had a very strong witness in our hearts that God wanted us there. After a while, I was given the opportunity to start a Thursday morning Women's Meeting at the church, Life Christian Center. This meeting was ordained by God as the next phase of my ministry, and *it was God's timing*.

As He blessed, it grew. At its peak, we enjoyed an attendance of four hundred ladies each week. Eventually I worked full-time at the church and became an

Associate Pastor there. I was ordained through Life Christian Center and taught Bible college there. The church then sponsored my first radio program which aired in St. Louis.

I learned many important lessons during my five years there. One thing I learned was how to submit to authority. A person is not fit to be in authority until they have experienced coming under authority. Remember, submission is not just an action, it is an attitude. You may decide to do what you are told, but a submissive attitude must be birthed in you, especially if you are strong-willed like I was.

Over a period of time I learned to work with a group of people and to function in various types of ministry. I also learned a lot more about waiting. There were many things God had put in my heart, things I wanted to do, but, once again, the time was not right — so more waiting, more learning and more growing.

These were great years, and they were hard years filled with laughter and tears, excitement and disappointment. Through it all, the pastors of Life Christian Center, Rick and Donna Shelton, and Dave and I became, and still are, the best of friends. We all grew together.

I have learned that when people grow together, if they do not give up on each other, they are usually meshed together in a deep relationship that will endure for all time. You might say that while the mess is being mashed out of you, you are being meshed together.

When Life Christian Center had grown to a congregation of about 1,200, the staff was preparing to move into their brand new, beautiful building. Everything was exploding with victory and excitement when God spoke again.

6

....

The Separation

Life In The Word Begins

Remember when God originally spoke to me? "The call" came while I was making my bed, and the Lord said, "You will go all over the place . . . and have a large teaching tape ministry." That had been fulfilled in a small way during the years of preparation, but the vision had increased in other areas.

One day in prayer, a specific Scripture was enlightened to me in Philippians 2:16 (AMP) in a mighty way. It said, "Holding out [to it]" (the world) "and offering [to all men] the Word of Life . . . ." That day I received a vision to reach out to the entire nation by radio.

I was not on any radio station at the time the vision came. I had traveled a little but not very far. There was much more in my heart, but I kept thinking God would somehow work all of it into my job at Life Christian Center, which I liked very much. But God had other plans.

Proverbs 16:9 (AMP) says, "A man's mind plans his way, but the Lord directs his steps." I had a plan. I thought it was God's plan, but He spoke again and said, "I am finished with you here. Take your ministry and go North, South, East, and West." I saw in the Spirit that I was to take the existing Life In The Word meeting that operated out of Life Christian Center and begin similar meetings in other places. I fought this for a long time, but I finally felt sure it was God saying to do it. I also knew that if I was wrong, I would lose everything the last ten years represented. I was afraid!

I finally obeyed God and left my job at the church. It was during this transition that God showed me that He was now separating me to "the call" on my life. Everything else had been wonderful, but it was all preparation. Each step of the way, God's anointing increased as my responsibility increased.

In Acts 13:2 (AMP) it is recorded that as the saints "were worshipping" together, the Holy Spirit told them to separate "now" Paul and Barnabas unto Him for the work to which He had called them. They had been doing things in ministry, fruitful things that brought blessing. But in God's timing, He said, "NOW is the appointed time."

I want you to be encouraged that in God's time you will see the dreams and visions that God has given you fulfilled. If He has placed a certain call on your life, He will fulfill it in His timing. Cooperate each step of the way and remember that the call, the anointing, and the separation to the call can occur over a span of many years. *Be faithful in all the little things. Your times are in His hands.*

7

....

Are You Tired of Waiting?

If you have been waiting a long time and have not seen much progress, you are probably getting very tired of waiting. I want to encourage you to take a fresh attitude toward waiting. The Bible, in Mark 4:20-27, says that we are to be patient like the farmer who puts his seed in the ground and then waits for the early and latter rain. The Word goes on to say that while he waits for the seed to sprout, he rises up and goes to bed, and eventually it comes up. And he, the farmer, knows not how.

God has taught me through these Scriptures to keep living the life I have now while I am waiting for things that are in my heart to come to pass. We can become so intent on trying to birth the next thing that we do not take care of and enjoy the things at hand.

I had a vision from God ten years before I began to see its fullness. During those ten years, I believe I missed a lot of joy trying to give birth outside of God's timing.

Let's say a woman who has five children becomes pregnant. If she started trying to give birth to the new baby in the first month, it would seem rather ridiculous. What if she tried so hard to get the new baby to come that she failed to take proper care of the five she already had? We can readily see the foolishness of this scenario. However, in reality, people often do the same thing with other situations.

Enjoy where you are while you are waiting to get to where you want to be! When the Bible says the farmer rises up and goes to bed, I believe it means he lives his ordinary, everyday life while he is waiting for his envisioned garden to sprout.

One day a pastor picked us up at a crowded airport. It was extremely busy. The escalators had lines, and the restaurants had lines. It seemed as if everywhere we turned we were waiting. I could see that the pastor was getting a bit frustrated with the whole thing. Suddenly he turned to me and said, "I guess you can see that I don't wait well."

Anytime we haven't learned to wait well the results are obvious, not only in the way we behave emotionally but also in our physical bodies. Waiting is a large part of life, and if waiting always brings frustration, it creates stress that eventually takes a toll on the physical body and can cause sickness. This particular pastor who did not "wait well" was very sick at the time with physical weakness that his doctor said had been produced by years of stress. *Take a new attitude toward waiting, and it will not have to be so difficult for you.*

In all truth we spend more time waiting in our lives than we do receiving.

After we receive what we are waiting for, we will begin waiting for something else. If you can see what I mean, you will be able to quickly realize that *waiting is a major part of life*.

Let's say you get a raise and then wait for the next one. You wait for a child, then you wait for them to get out of diapers into pants and soon you are waiting for them to be able to buy their own pants! You wait to buy a house, then wait to buy furniture for your house that you are no longer waiting for. Then you wait to be able to afford a cleaning lady to help you clean your house and the furniture that you waited for. Do you get my meaning?

Learn to enjoy waiting, realizing that waiting is what will deliver your dream. I really should say "waiting well" is what will deliver your dream. The fulfillment, of course, comes from God, but waiting is like the delivery boy. Sometimes a person starts waiting, and by the time the delivery boy arrives, they have gone off and started something else, and they probably will not be around for the end fulfillment of that thing either.

Impatient people often do not hang around long enough to see the finish of really great things because great things take so much time to mature. My husband, Dave, always says, *"Fast and fragile; slow and solid."* If it is thrown together quickly to suit the impatient and those who do not wait well, it is not likely to be lasting. However, if people are willing to wait on God's perfect timing, it will be put together right and will last a long, long time.

Occasionally we see "shooting stars" in ministry – people who come out of seemingly nowhere and practically overnight are known worldwide, usually because they happened to get in with a certain group of people who had an ability to open doors for them. Rarely do their ministries last. They often get into trouble financially or morally because character is built during the hard times of waiting, but they didn't go through that character-building time.

If a person somehow avoids all the hard things and shoots up overnight, they generally do not last. Mark 4:5, 6 says that the seed which shoots up overnight withers when the heat comes. When we finally learn to respect and appreciate the times of waiting, God goes to work in earnest. And even though we cannot see what is happening, the things that will make us happy later on are happening right now behind the scenes.

8

....

Patience, Please!

The Bible says in Hebrews 6:12 that we inherit the promises through faith and patience. Now inheritance does not require any effort on our part. It only requires waiting until the appointed time. For example, you may believe, or have faith, that a relative has willed you an inheritance, but you must have patience and wait for the proper time to receive it. Faith and patience are partners. They work together to bring the desired result.

James 1:2, 3 (AMP) says that we are to be joyful when we "encounter trials of any sort" knowing that "the proving of your faith" brings out patience. And when patience has had her perfect work, we will be a people "perfectly and fully developed . . . lacking in nothing." Wow! What a Scripture!

The Greek word for "patience" in this verse, hupomone, means the kind of "patience which grows only in trial."[1] In other words, how can we grow in patience unless we are required to wait for something we want or endure something we do not want while we are waiting?

When we have trials, we grow, or at least we can grow, if we "let patience have her perfect work" (James 1:4). Resistance, bitterness, and running away from every hard place does not produce patience. James 1:4 (AMP) says that we can be perfectly developed and lacking in (or "wanting nothing" KJV) once patience has done a thorough work. This is simple to see. If a person is totally patient, he or she can be peaceful and joyful in any situation.

I am certainly not perfect in patience, but I have grown a lot. There was a time when I was extremely

---

[1]W. E. Vine, *An Expository Dictionary of New Testament Words* (Old Tappan, New Jersey: Fleming H. Revell Co., 1940), Vol. III, p. 167.

impatient, and I did not wait well. I finally realized that God was not going to change, so I decided I had better change and adapt to His ways. He says that we receive by faith and patience, so I decided to let patience develop in me. *I have grown in patience, and at an equal rate, I have gained peace and joy.*

Patience is a fruit of the Spirit. Patience is a powerful witness to unbelievers. It is like a muscle – the more you need to use it, the stronger it gets. Then finally, it is fully developed, and you only have to do exercises to keep yourself toned up in the area of patience – various and sundry things that do not happen as planned like slow people in front of you, a stalled car on the highway, not understanding what is happening in your life or needing answers that seem slow in coming.

All of these things help us in the end, even though they are hard when we are going through them. If we can see this, it will give us a new appreciation for patience. Hebrews 12:1 (AMP) encourages us saying, "Let us run with patient endurance and steady and active persistence the appointed course of the race that is set before us." Every race has a finish line. You will cross the finish line, but Hebrews tells us how to run the race.

Be Patient With Yourself

Allow me to encourage you to begin building a foundation for a patient lifestyle by being patient with yourself. When you make mistakes, receive mercy from God and press on toward the finish line. Be patient with yourself while you are overcoming your weaknesses. *Impatience breeds frustration*, and frustration moves us into a realm of emotions which are unstable, then we end up making more mistakes than if we had given ourselves some patience in the first place.

People improve more rapidly under patience than under pressure! Be generous with patience. Give it away freely to yourself and others. You will find the benefits delightful. Luke 8:15 (AMP) says, "steadily bring forth fruit with patience."

....

When Will My Dream Come True?

Your dream is in the process right now! It is on the stove cooking. You have heard the phrase, "The watched pot never boils." I really encourage you to simply get the most out of every day. Do your part, but do not try to do God's part.

There is a perfect timing – God's timing. Only He knows when it is. Honor God by trusting Him, and while you are traveling the road to fulfillment, *enjoy the trip!*

No one can tell you exactly when it will come, but be assured it will come at just the right time.

Believe it, and enter God's rest!

Is 40:29-31

Experiencing a New Life

If you have never invited Jesus to be your Lord and Savior, I invite you to do so now. You can pray this prayer, and if you are really sincere about it, you will experience a new life in Christ.

Father God, I believe Jesus Christ is your Son, the Savior of the world. I believe He died on the cross for me, and He bore all of my sins. He went to hell in my place and triumphed over death and the grave. I believe Jesus was resurrected from the dead and is now seated at your right hand. I need You, Jesus. Forgive my sins, save me, come to live inside me. I want to be born again.

Now believe Jesus is living in your heart. You are forgiven and made righteous, and when Jesus comes, you will go to heaven.

Find a good church that is teaching God's Word and begin to grow in Christ. Nothing will change in your life without knowledge of God's Word.

Beloved,

John 8:31, 32 (AMP) says, "If you abide in My word . . . you are truly My disciples. And you will know the Truth, and the Truth will set you free."

I exhort you to take hold of God's Word, plant it deep in your heart, and according to 2 Corinthians 3:18, as you look into the Word, you will be transformed into the image of Jesus Christ.

Write and let me know you have accepted Jesus, and ask for a free booklet on how to begin your new life in Christ.

With Love,
Joyce

About the Author

Joyce Meyer has been teaching the Word of God since 1976 and in full-time ministry since 1980. As an associate pastor at Life Christian Center in St. Louis, Missouri, she developed, coordinated and taught a weekly meeting known as "Life In The Word." After more than five years, the Lord brought it to a conclusion, directing her to establish her own ministry and call it "Life In The Word, Inc."

Joyce's "Life In The Word" radio and television programs are heard or seen throughout the United States and the world. Her teaching tapes are enjoyed internationally. She travels extensively conducting Life In The Word conferences.

Joyce and her husband, Dave, business administrator at Life In The Word, have been married for over 33 years and are the parents of four children. All four children are married, and along with their spouses, work with Dave and Joyce in the ministry. Joyce and Dave reside in Fenton, Missouri, a St. Louis suburb.

Joyce believes the call on her life is to establish believers in God's Word. She says, "Jesus died to set the captives free, and far too many Christians have little or no victory in their daily lives." Finding herself in the same situation many years ago, and having found freedom to live in victory through applying God's Word, Joyce goes equipped to set captives free and to exchange *ashes for beauty*. Joyce believes that every person who walks in victory leads many others into victory.

Joyce has taught on emotional healing and related subjects in meetings all over the country, helping multiplied thousands. She has recorded more than 200 different audiocassette albums and is the author of 34 books to help the Body of Christ on various topics.

Her "Emotional Healing Package" contains over 23 hours of teaching on the subject. Albums included in this package are: "Confidence"; "Beauty for Ashes" (includes a syllabus); "Managing Your

Emotions"; "Bitterness, Resentment, and Unforgiveness"; "Root of Rejection"; and a 90-minute Scripture/music tape entitled "Healing the Brokenhearted."

Joyce's "Mind Package" features five different audio tape series on the subject of the mind. They include: "Mental Strongholds and Mindsets"; "Wilderness Mentality"; "The Mind of the Flesh"; "The Wandering, Wondering Mind"; and "Mind, Mouth, Moods & Attitudes." The package also contains Joyce's powerful 288-page book, *Battlefield of the Mind*. On the subject of love she has two tape series entitled, "Love Is..." and "Love: The Ultimate Power."

Write to Joyce Meyer's office for a resource catalog and further information on how to obtain the tapes you need to bring total healing to your life.

To contact the author write:

Joyce Meyer
Life In The Word, Inc.
P. O. Box 655
Fenton, Missouri 63026
or call:
(636) 349-0303

Internet Address:
www.jmministries.org

*Please include your testimony
or help received from this
book when you write.
Your prayer requests are welcome.*

In Canada, please write:
Joyce Meyer Ministries Canada, Inc.
Lambeth Box 1300
London, ON N6P 1T5

In Australia, please write:
Joyce Meyer Ministries-Australia
Locked Bag 77
Mansfield Delivery Centre
Queensland 4122
or call:
(07) 3349 1200

Books By Joyce Meyer

How to Succeed at Being Yourself

Eat and Stay Thin

Weary Warriors, Fainting Saints

Life in the Word Journal

Life in the Word Devotional

Be Anxious for Nothing —
The Art of Casting Your Cares and Resting in God

The Help Me! Series:
I'm Alone!
I'm Stressed! · I'm Insecure!
I'm Discouraged! · I'm Depressed!
I'm Worried! · I'm Afraid!

Don't Droad
Overcoming the Spirit of Dread
with the Supernatural Power of God

Managing Your Emotions
Instead of Your Emotions Managing You

Life in the Word (Quotes)

Healing the Brokenhearted

"Me and My Big Mouth!"

Prepare to Prosper

Do It! Afraid

Expect a Move of God in Your Life...Suddenly

Enjoying Where You Are on the
Way to Where You Are Going
The Most Important Decision You'll Ever Make
When, God, When?
Why, God, Why?
The Word, the Name, the Blood
Battlefield of the Mind
Tell Them I Love Them
Peace
The Root of Rejection
Beauty for Ashes
If Not for the Grace of God

By Dave Meyer
Nuggets of Life

Available from your local bookstore.

Harrison House
Tulsa, Oklahoma 74153

The Harrison House Vision

Proclaiming the truth and the power
Of the Gospel of Jesus Christ
With excellence;

Challenging Christians to
Live victoriously,
Grow spiritually,
Know God intimately.